U.S.

MARINE CORPS

BY NICK GORDON

BELLWETHER MEDIA · MINNEAPOLIS, MN

EPIC BOOKS are no ordinary books. They burst with intense action, high-speed heroics, and shadows of the unknown. Are you ready for an Epic adventure?

This edition first published in 2013 by Bellwether Media, Inc.

No part of this publication may be reproduced in whole or in part without written permission of the publisher. For information regarding permission, write to Bellwether Media, Inc., Attention: Permissions Department, 5357 Penn Avenue South, Minneapolis, MN 55419.

Library of Congress Cataloging-in-Publication Data

Gordon, Nick.
  U.S. Marine Corps / by Nick Gordon.
    p. cm. – (Epic books: U.S. Military)
  Includes bibliographical references and index.
  Summary: "Engaging images accompany information about the U.S. Marine Corps. The combination of high-interest subject matter and light text is intended for students in grades 2 through 7"–Provided by publisher.
  Audience: Grades 2-7.
  ISBN 978-1-60014-829-3 (hbk. : alk. paper)
  1. United States. Marine Corps–Juvenile literature. I. Title.
  VE23.G67 2013
  359.9'60973–dc23   2012008562

Printed in the United States of America, North Mankato, MN.

A special thanks to Ted Carlson/Fotodynamics for contributing images.

TABLE OF CONTENTS

THE U.S. MARINE CORPS

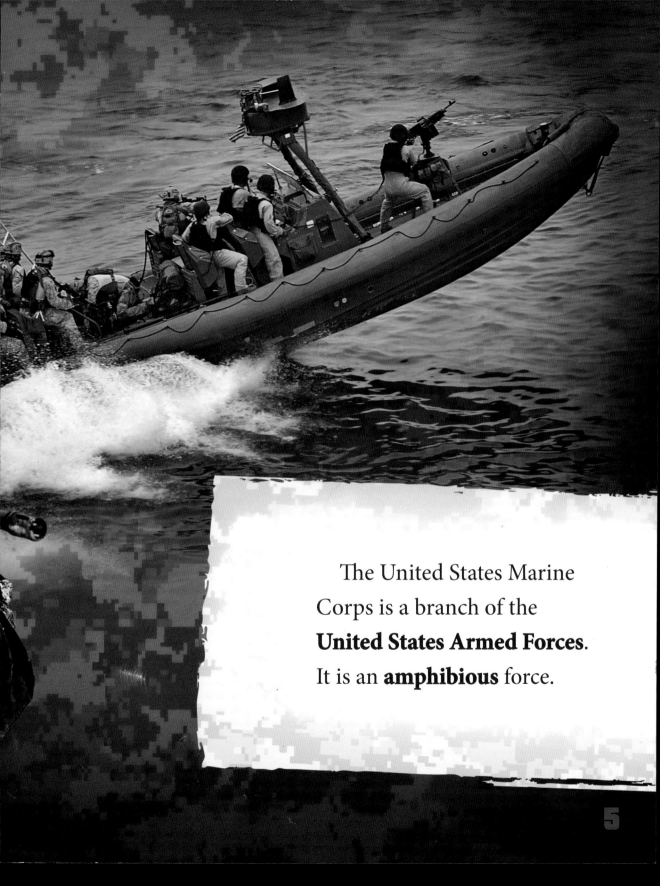

The United States Marine Corps is a branch of the **United States Armed Forces**. It is an **amphibious** force.

UNITED STATES MARINE CORPS

Founded:	**1775**
Headquarters:	**Arlington, Virginia**
Motto:	***Semper Fidelis* (Always Faithful)**
Size:	**More than 200,000 active personnel**
Major Engagements:	**Revolutionary War, War of 1812, American Civil War, World War I, World War II, Korean War, Vietnam War, Gulf War, Iraq War, War on Terror**

The Marine Corps works closely with the United States Navy. Navy ships often carry Marines into battle.

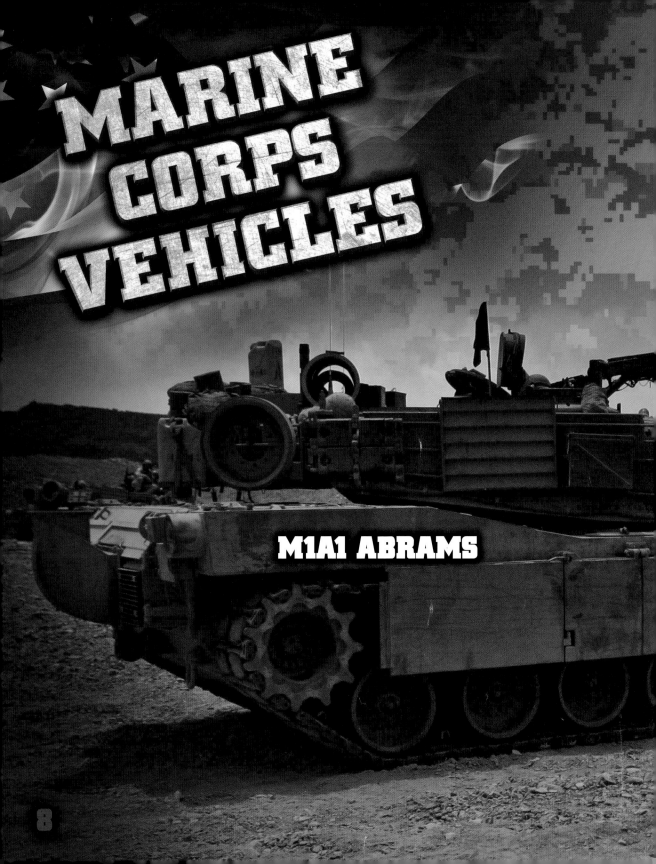

MARINE CORPS VEHICLES

M1A1 ABRAMS

Marines use many vehicles. The M1A1 Abrams is a main battle tank. It has a large gun and strong **armor**.

AAV-7A1

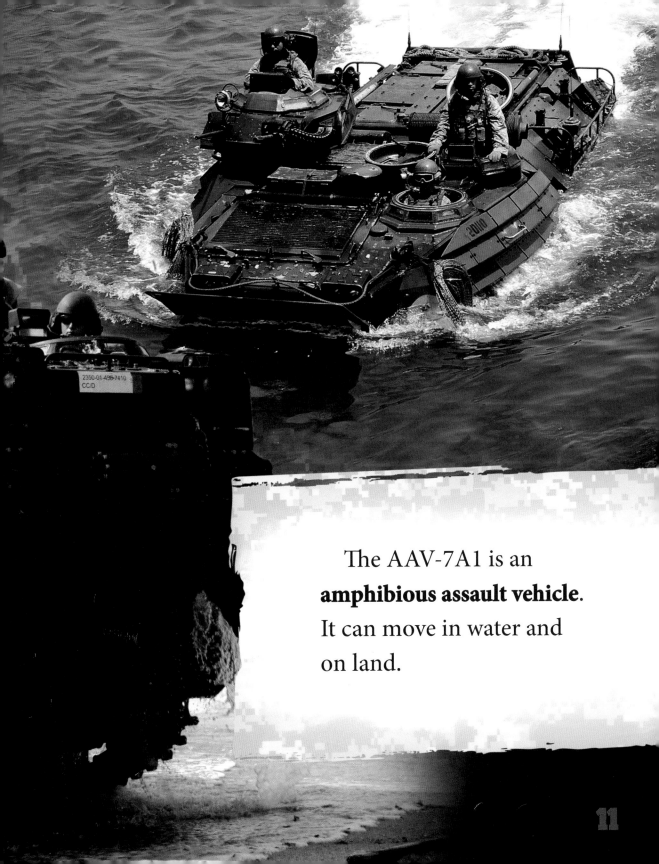

The AAV-7A1 is an **amphibious assault vehicle**. It can move in water and on land.

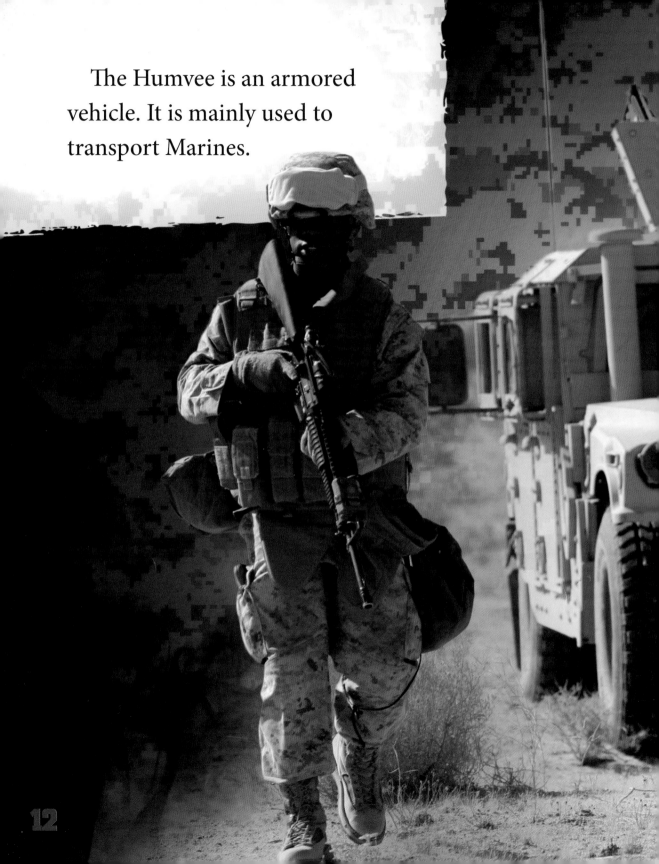

The Humvee is an armored vehicle. It is mainly used to transport Marines.

HUMVEE

MV-22 OSPREY

AH-1 SUPER COBRA

Marines also use aircraft. The MV-22 Osprey is a **tilt-rotor** aircraft. It can take off and land like a helicopter.

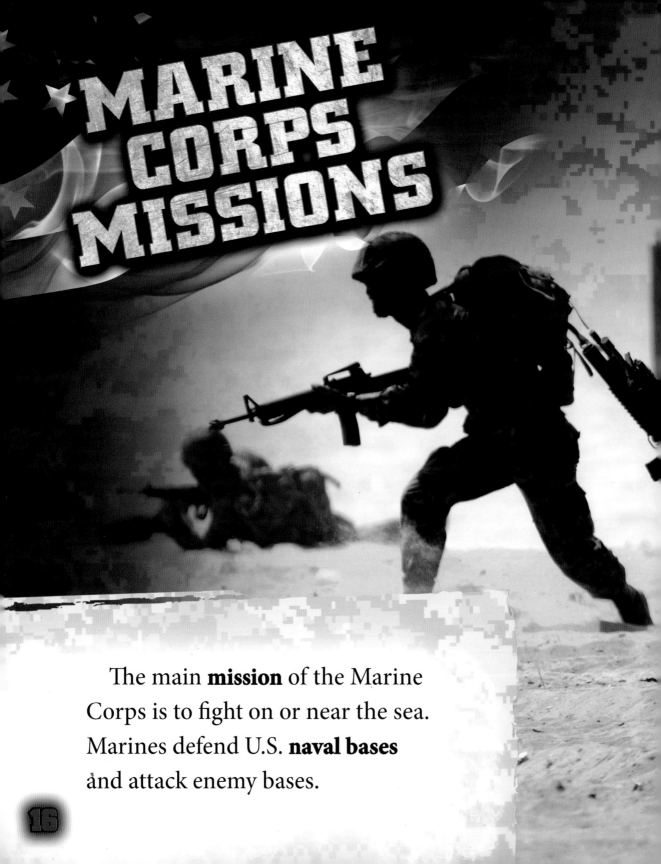

MARINE CORPS MISSIONS

The main **mission** of the Marine Corps is to fight on or near the sea. Marines defend U.S. **naval bases** and attack enemy bases.

The Marines are also an **expeditionary force**. They are sent far from base to collect **intelligence** and wage war.

MARINE FACT

Marines fought pirates off
the coast of North Africa
in the 1800s.

The Marine Corps **motto** is *Semper Fidelis*. This means "Always Faithful." Marines remain faithful to their mission, their country, and one another.

GLOSSARY

amphibious—able to move through water and on land

amphibious assault vehicle—a vehicle designed to carry troops through water and on land

armor—thick plates that cover a vehicle to protect its crew

expeditionary force—a combat unit trained to fight far from its home base

intelligence—information about the enemy

mission—a military task

motto—a short phrase that shows the beliefs and goals of a group

naval bases—military bases where ships, aircraft, and personnel are stationed

tilt-rotor—a type of aircraft with two spinning rotors; the rotors can be tilted up like a helicopter's or forward like an airplane's.

United States Armed Forces—the five branches of the United States military; they are the Air Force, the Army, the Coast Guard, the Marine Corps, and the Navy.

TO LEARN MORE

At the Library

Alvarez, Carlos. *Marine Expeditionary Units*. Minneapolis, Minn.: Bellwether Media, 2010.

Gordon, Nick. *U.S. Navy*. Minneapolis, Minn.: Bellwether Media, 2013.

Schwartz, Heather E. *Women of the U.S. Marine Corps: Breaking Barriers*. Mankato, Minn.: Capstone Press, 2011.

On the Web

Learning more about the
U.S. Marine Corps is as easy as 1, 2, 3.

1. Go to www.factsurfer.com.

2. Enter "U.S. Marine Corps" into the search box.

3. Click the "Surf" button and you will see a list
of related Web sites.

With factsurfer.com, finding more information
is just a click away.

INDEX